Look, a Ray!

by Tessa Kenan

BUMBA BOOKS™

LERNER PUBLICATIONS ◆ MINNEAPOLIS

Note to Educators:

Throughout this book, you'll find critical thinking questions. These can be used to engage young readers in thinking critically about the topic and in using the text and photos to do so.

Lerner Publications Company
A division of Lerner Publishing Group, Inc.
241 First Avenue North
Minneapolis, MN 55401 USA

For reading levels and more information, look up this title at www.lernerbooks.com.

Library of Congress Cataloging-in-Publication Data

Names: Kenan, Tessa, author.
Title: Look, a ray! / by Tessa Kenan.
Description: Minneapolis : Lerner Publications, [2017] | Series: Bumba books—I see ocean animals | Audience: Age 4–8. | Audience: K to grade 3. | Includes bibliographical references and index.
Identifiers: LCCN 2016001060 (print) | LCCN 2016003113 (ebook) | ISBN 9781512414202 (lb : alk. paper) | ISBN 9781512415070 (pb : alk. paper) | ISBN 9781512415087 (eb pdf)
Subjects: LCSH: Rays (Fishes)—Juvenile literature. | Stingrays—Juvenile literature.
Classification: LCC QL638.8 .K46 2017 (print) | LCC QL638.8 (ebook) | DDC 597.3/5—dc23

LC record available at http://lccn.loc.gov/2016001060

Manufactured in the United States of America
1 – VP – 7/15/16

LERNER
SOURCE

Expand learning beyond the printed book. Download free, complementary educational resources for this book from our website, www.lernerresource.com.

Table of Contents

Rays Swim 4

Parts of a Ray 22

Picture Glossary 23

Index 24

Read More 24

Rays Swim

Rays are fish.

Rays swim in warm ocean waters.

There are more than five hundred kinds of rays.

Rays have two

large fins.

Rays flap their

fins to swim.

Rays have thin tails.

Some rays sting with their tails.

They sting sharks.

Sharks try to eat rays.

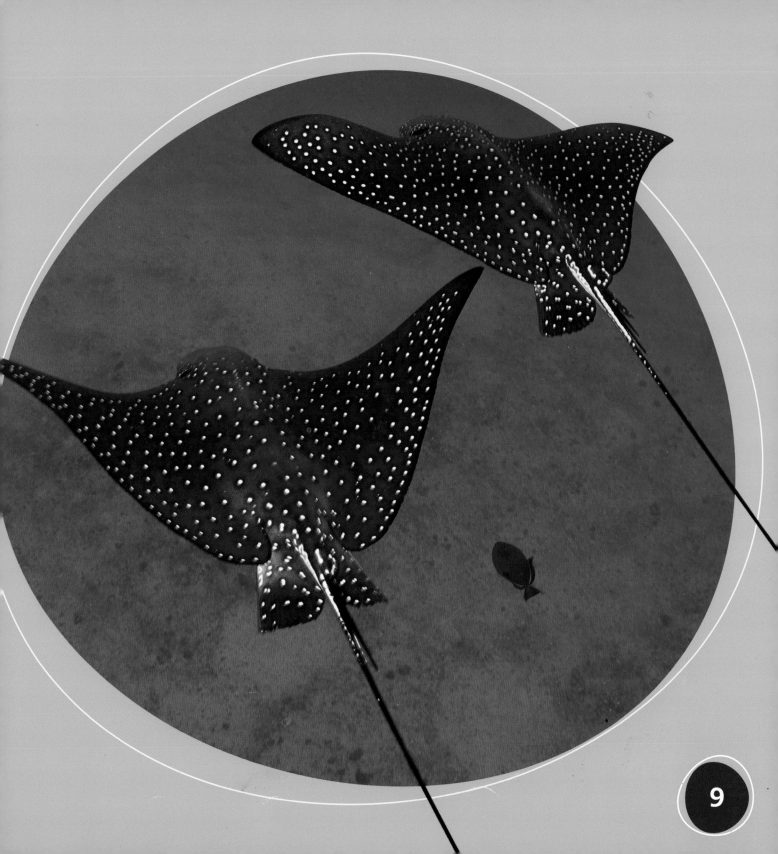

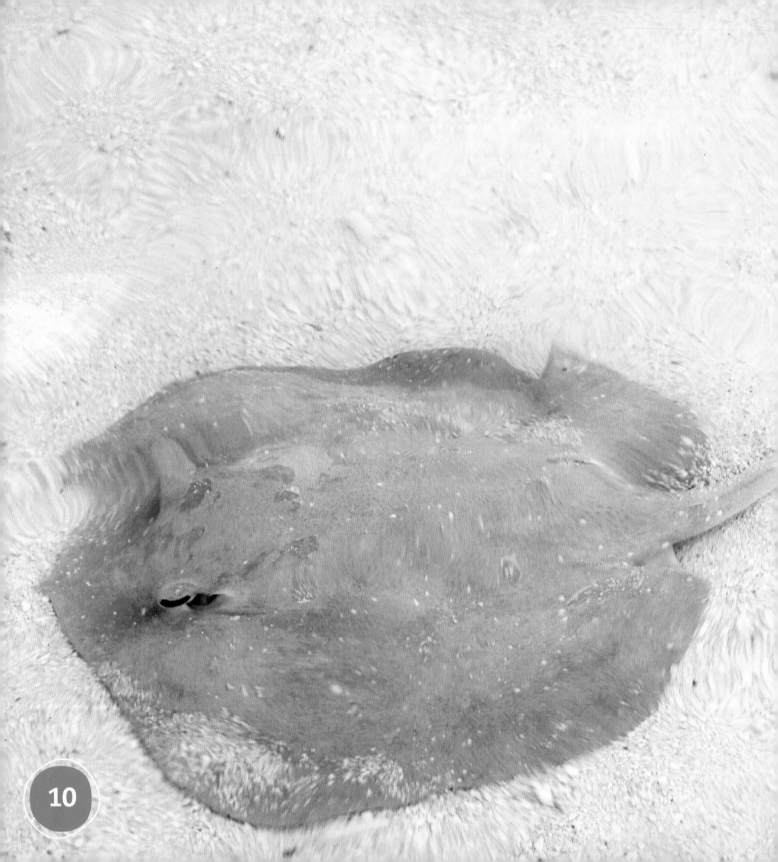

Rays hide in sand.
Their colors match
the sand.

**How might a
ray's color help
it stay safe?**

A ray has two eyes.

They are on the top of its body.

The mouth is on the bottom.

So are the gills.

Why would it be helpful to have the eyes on top?

Rays use their strong teeth to eat.

They can crack the shells of clams.

Baby rays are

called pups.

Mother rays have two

to six pups at a time.

16

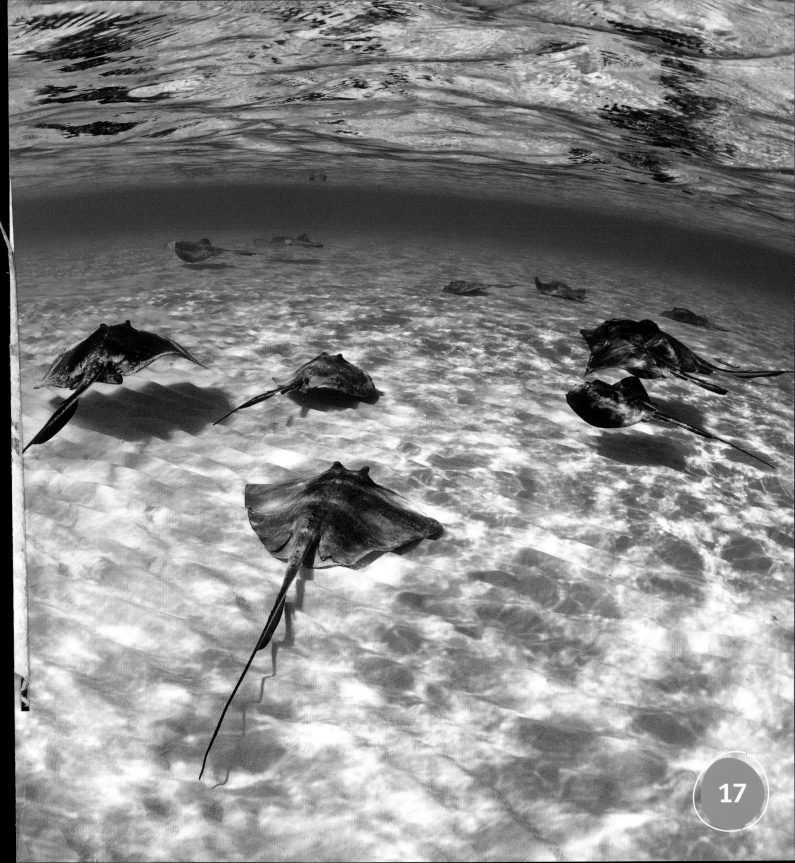

Some rays live alone.

Others swim together.

A group is called a school.

Why might rays swim in groups?

Some rays jump.

This manta ray is large.

It jumps high out of the water.

Parts of a Ray

eyes

mouth

gills

fins

tail

Picture Glossary

fins

body parts that help ocean animals swim

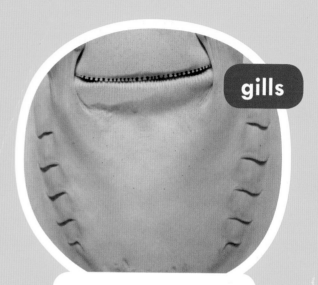

gills

body parts that help fish breathe

pups

baby rays

school

a group of rays

23

Index

colors, 11

eyes, 12

fins, 7

gills, 12

manta ray, 21

mouth, 12

ocean, 4

pups, 16

school, 19

sharks, 8

sting, 8

tails, 8

teeth, 15

Read More

Anderson, Sheila. *What Can Live in the Ocean?* Minneapolis: Lerner Publications, 2011.

Gerber, Carole. *Stingrays!: Underwater Fliers.* New York: Random House, 2015.

Meister, Cari. *Stingrays.* Minneapolis: Bullfrog Books, 2015.

Photo Credits